# Easy Design Adult Color By Number Jumbo Coloring Book of Large Print Flowers, Birds, and Butterflies

## By Laura's Dot to Dot Therapy

# Thank you
# for your purchase!

**Claim your FREE digital copy of our
Highlight Reel Color By Number Book:**

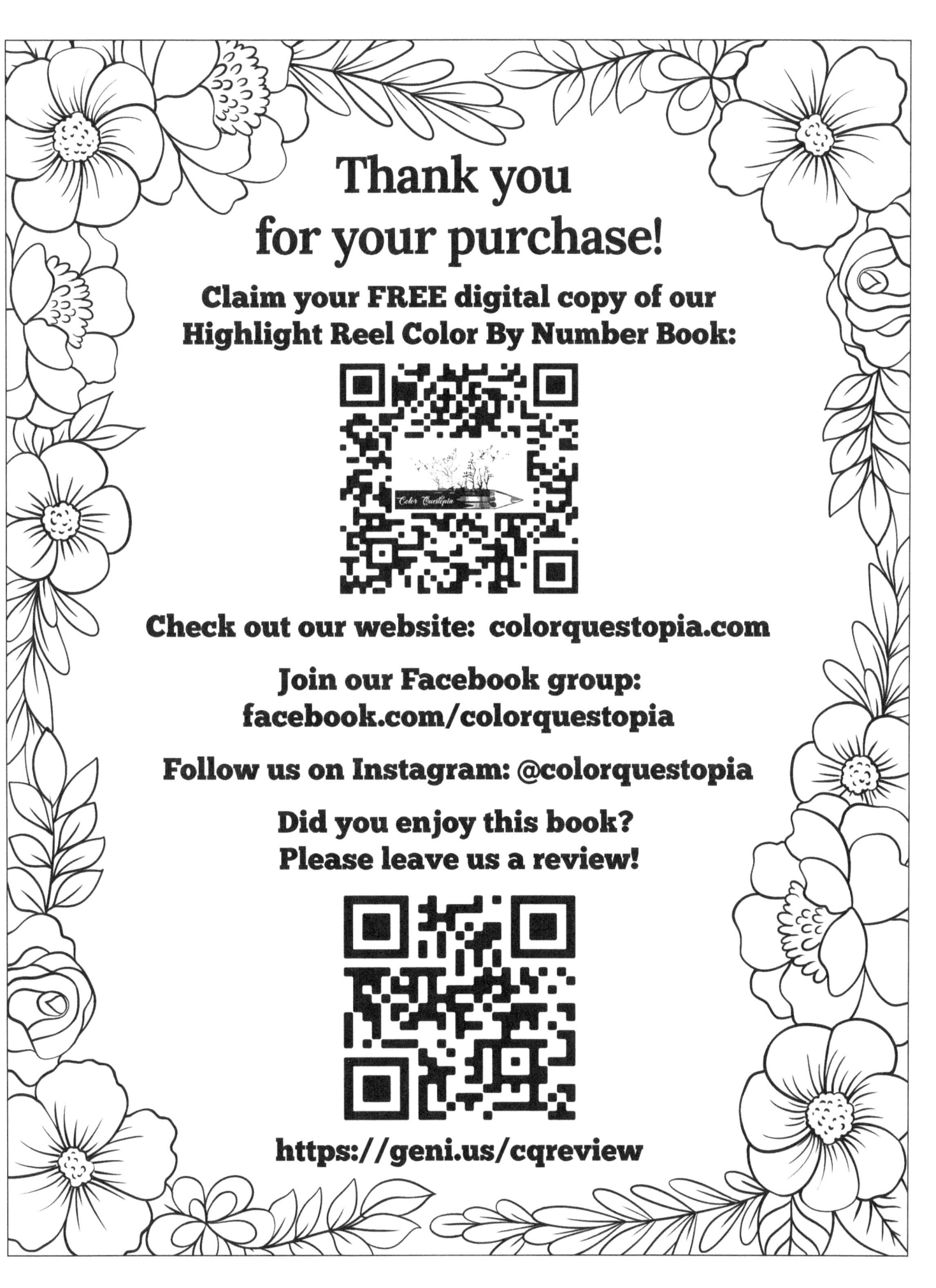

**Check out our website: colorquestopia.com**

**Join our Facebook group:
facebook.com/colorquestopia**

**Follow us on Instagram: @colorquestopia**

**Did you enjoy this book?
Please leave us a review!**

**https://geni.us/cqreview**

# Color By Number Tips

1. **Relax and have fun**
   Let your cares slip away as you color the images. Take your time. Coloring is a meditative activity and there's no wrong way to do it. Feel free to color as you listen to music, watch TV, lounge in bed- do whatever relaxes you most! You can also color while you're out and about- on the train or at a cafe- take the book with you anywhere you go. Coloring is therapeutic and is great for stress relief and relaxation!

2. **Colors corresponding to each number are shown on the back cover of the book**
   Each number corresponds to a color shown on the back of the book. You can match the color as closely as you like- but feel free to change the color or the shade if you don't have the exact color match- that's totally fine. Although this is a color by number book, it's completely okay to get creative and color the images with whichever colors you like and have. The numbers are there to be a guide and to allow you to color without having to focus your energy on choosing colors.

3. **Choose your coloring tools**
   Everyone has their favorite coloring markers, crayons, pencils, pens- even paints! Feel free to color with any tool that you like! If you choose markers or paints, we recommend putting a blank sheet of paper or cardboard behind each image, so that your colors don't run onto the next image.


   Enjoy!

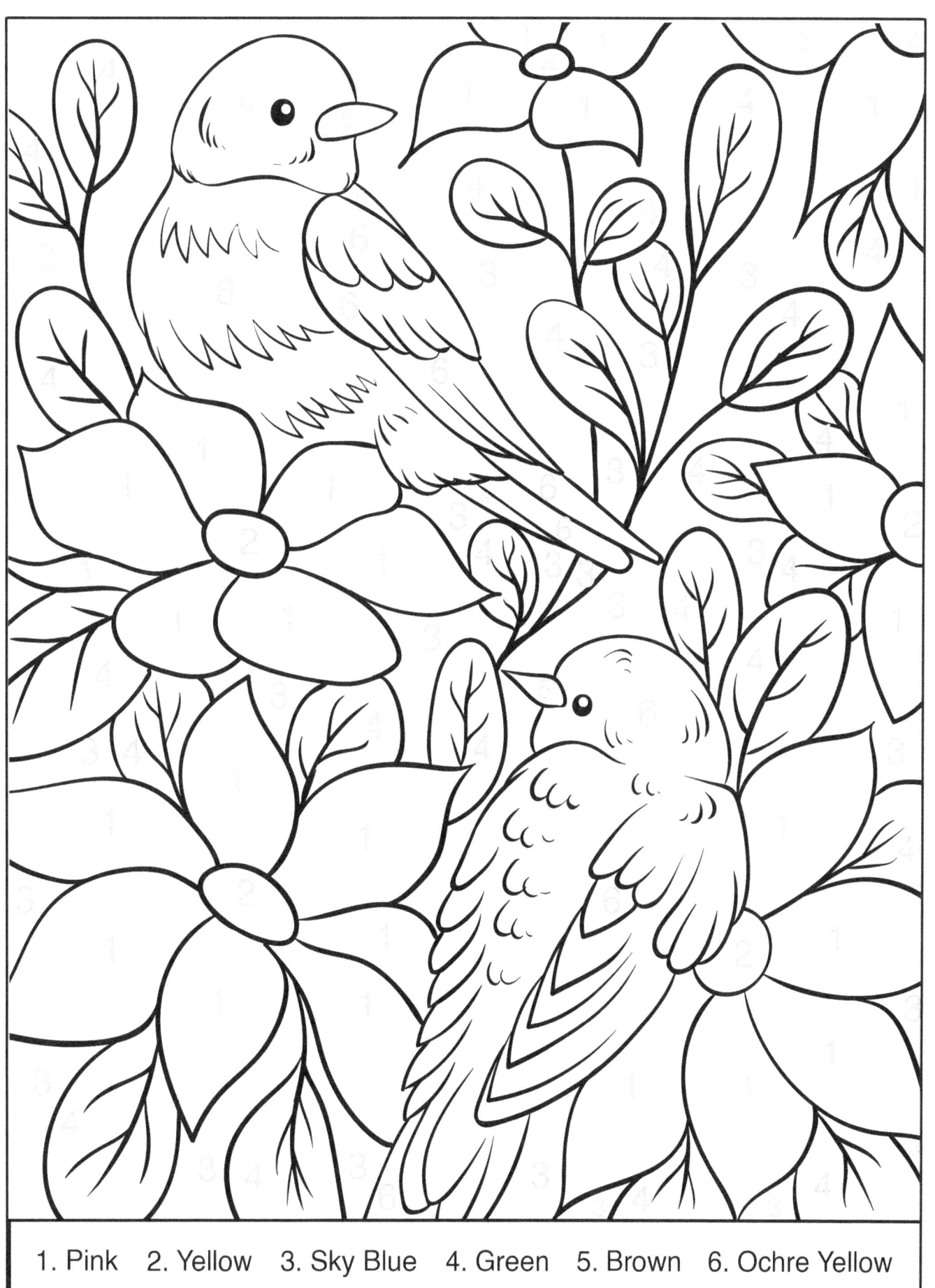

1. Pink   2. Yellow   3. Sky Blue   4. Green   5. Brown   6. Ochre Yellow

1. Pink    2. Yellow    3. Green    4. Red    5. Orange    6. Brown    7. Dark Blue    8. Light Green    9. Sky Blue    10. Purple    11. Light Pink    12. Violet

1. Pink   2. Yellow   3. Sky Blue   4. Green   5. Brown   6. Ochre Yellow
7. Dark Blue   8. Red   9. Medium Blue

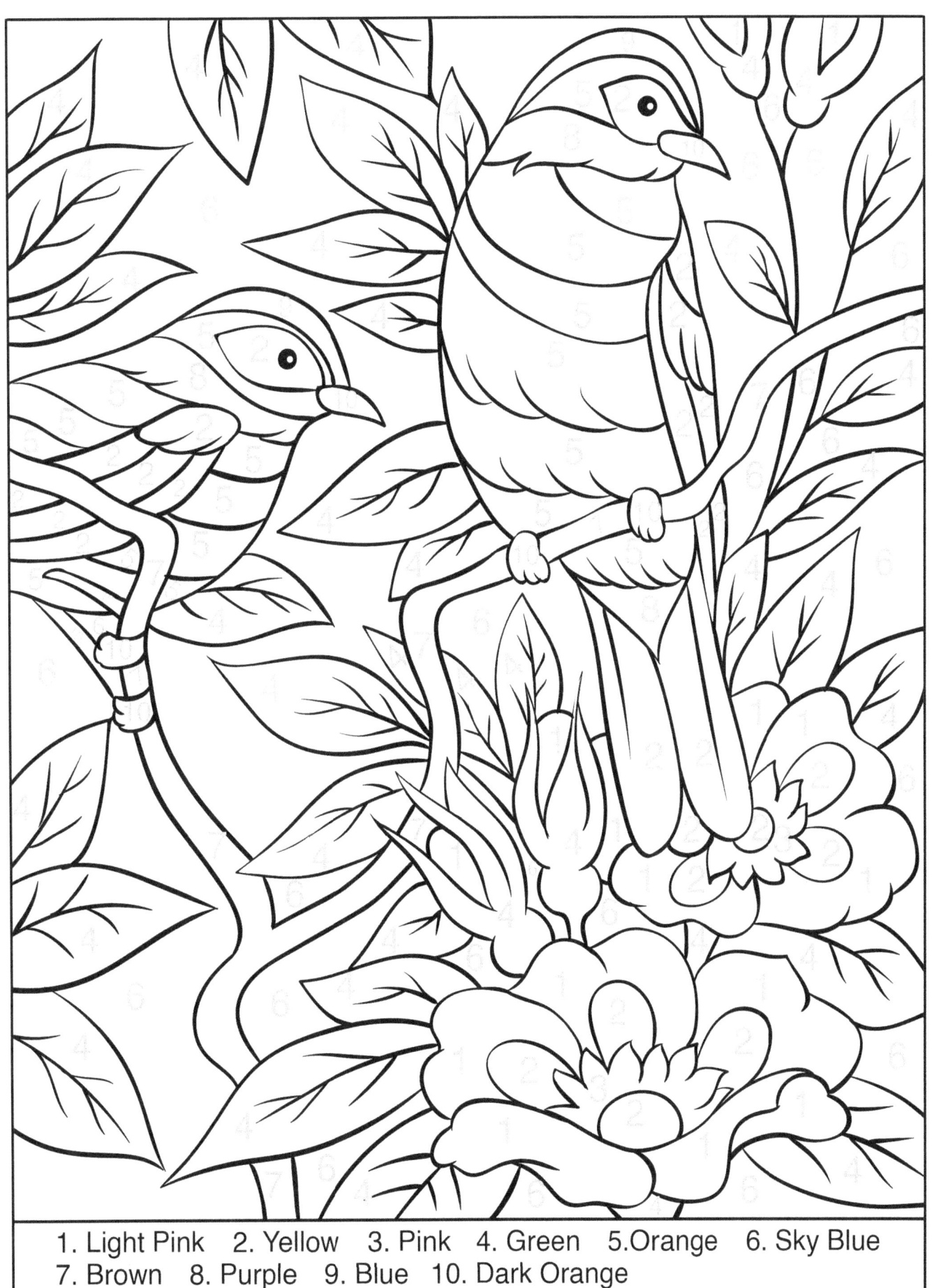

1. Light Pink   2. Yellow   3. Pink   4. Green   5.Orange   6. Sky Blue
7. Brown   8. Purple   9. Blue   10. Dark Orange

1. Pink   2. Yellow   3. Light Green   4. Red   5. Orange   6. Brown
7. Sky Blue   8. Purple   9. Dark Green

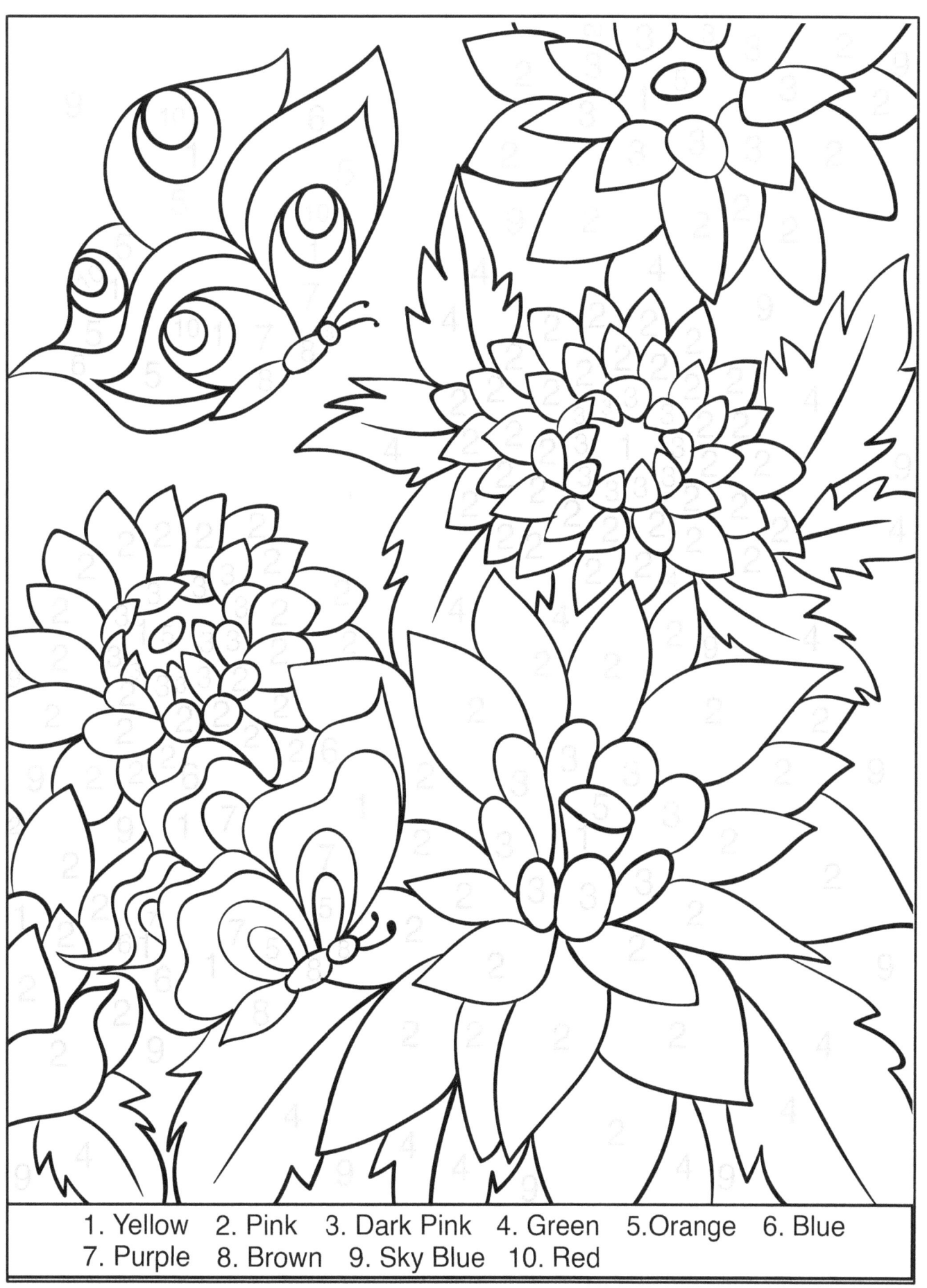

1. Yellow    2. Pink    3. Dark Pink    4. Green    5.Orange    6. Blue
7. Purple    8. Brown    9. Sky Blue    10. Red

1. Pink   2. Yellow   3. Green   4. Red   5.Orange   6. Dark Blue
7. Brown   8. Sky Blue   9. Purple   10. Light Pink

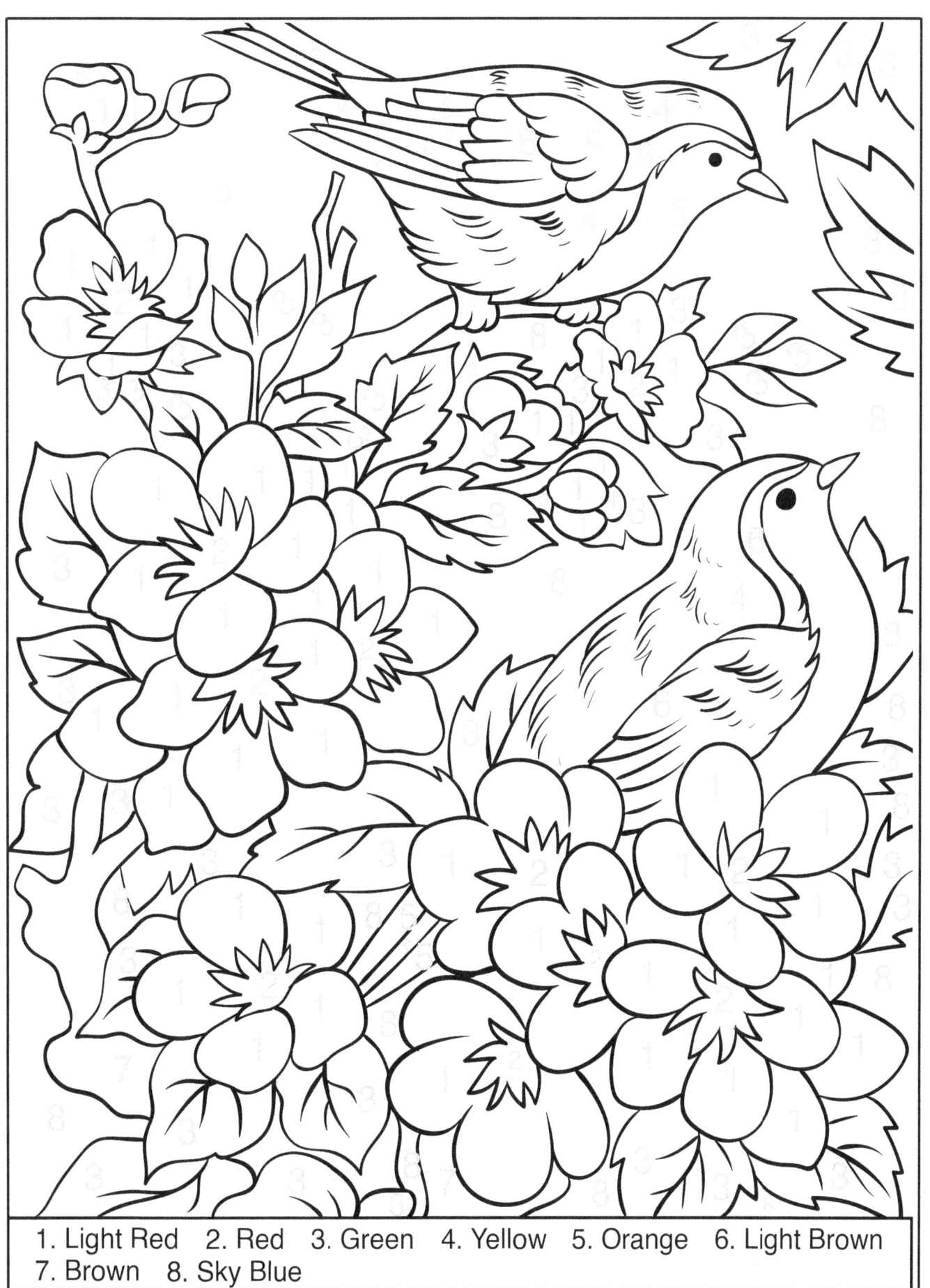

1. Light Red   2. Red   3. Green   4. Yellow   5. Orange   6. Light Brown
7. Brown   8. Sky Blue

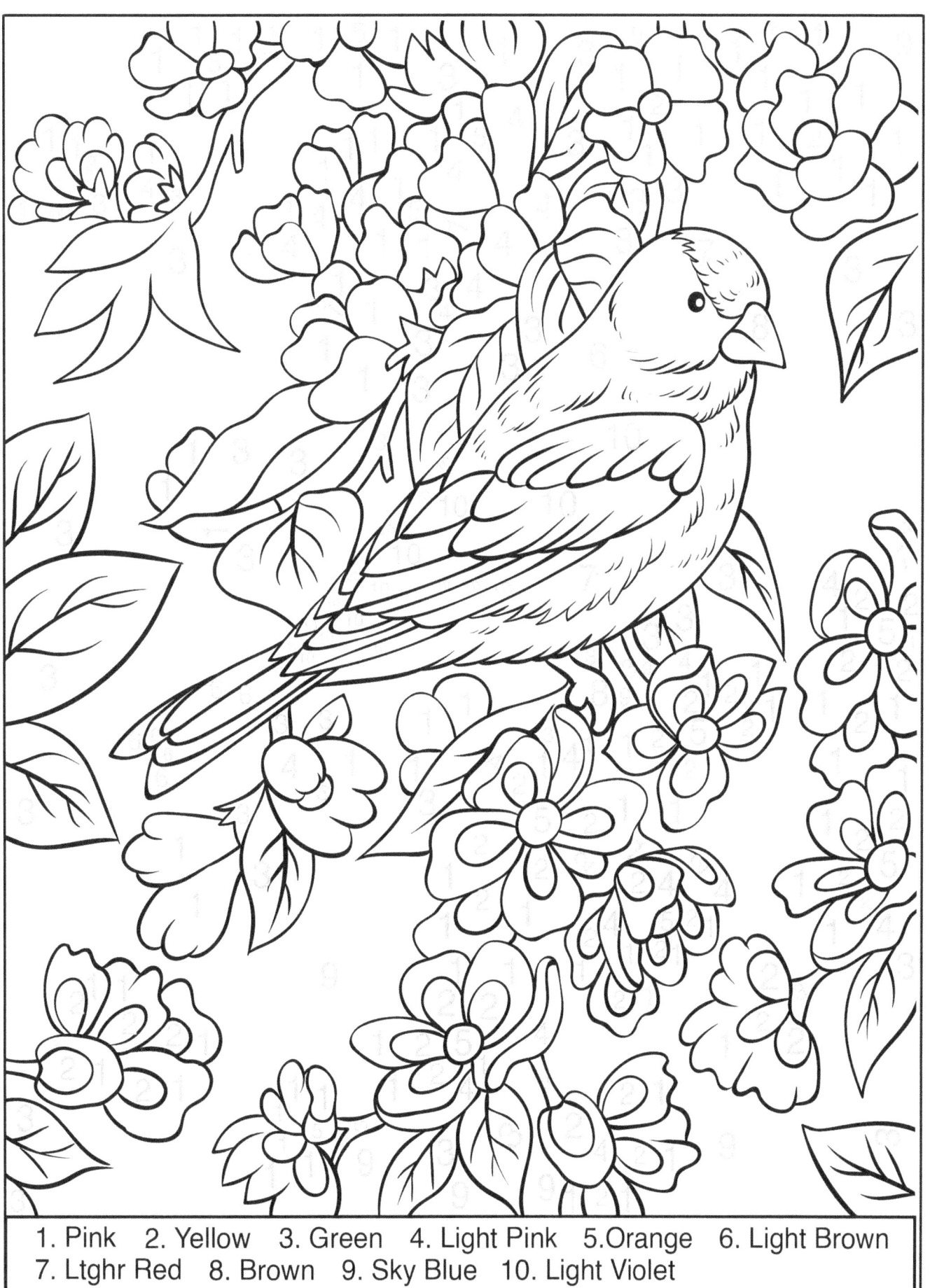

1. Pink   2. Yellow   3. Green   4. Light Pink   5.Orange   6. Light Brown
7. Ltghr Red   8. Brown   9. Sky Blue   10. Light Violet

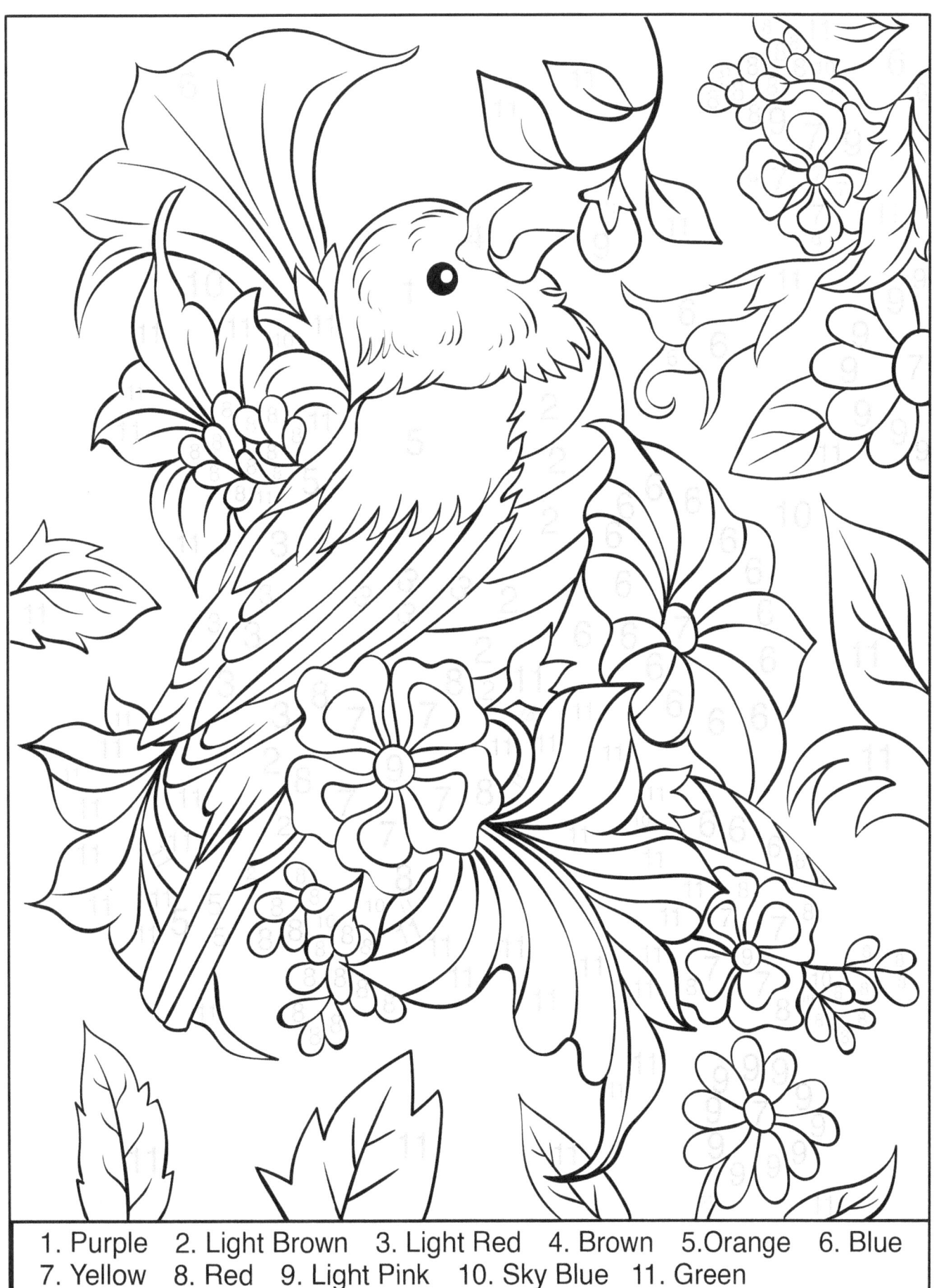

1. Purple   2. Light Brown   3. Light Red   4. Brown   5.Orange   6. Blue
7. Yellow   8. Red   9. Light Pink   10. Sky Blue   11. Green

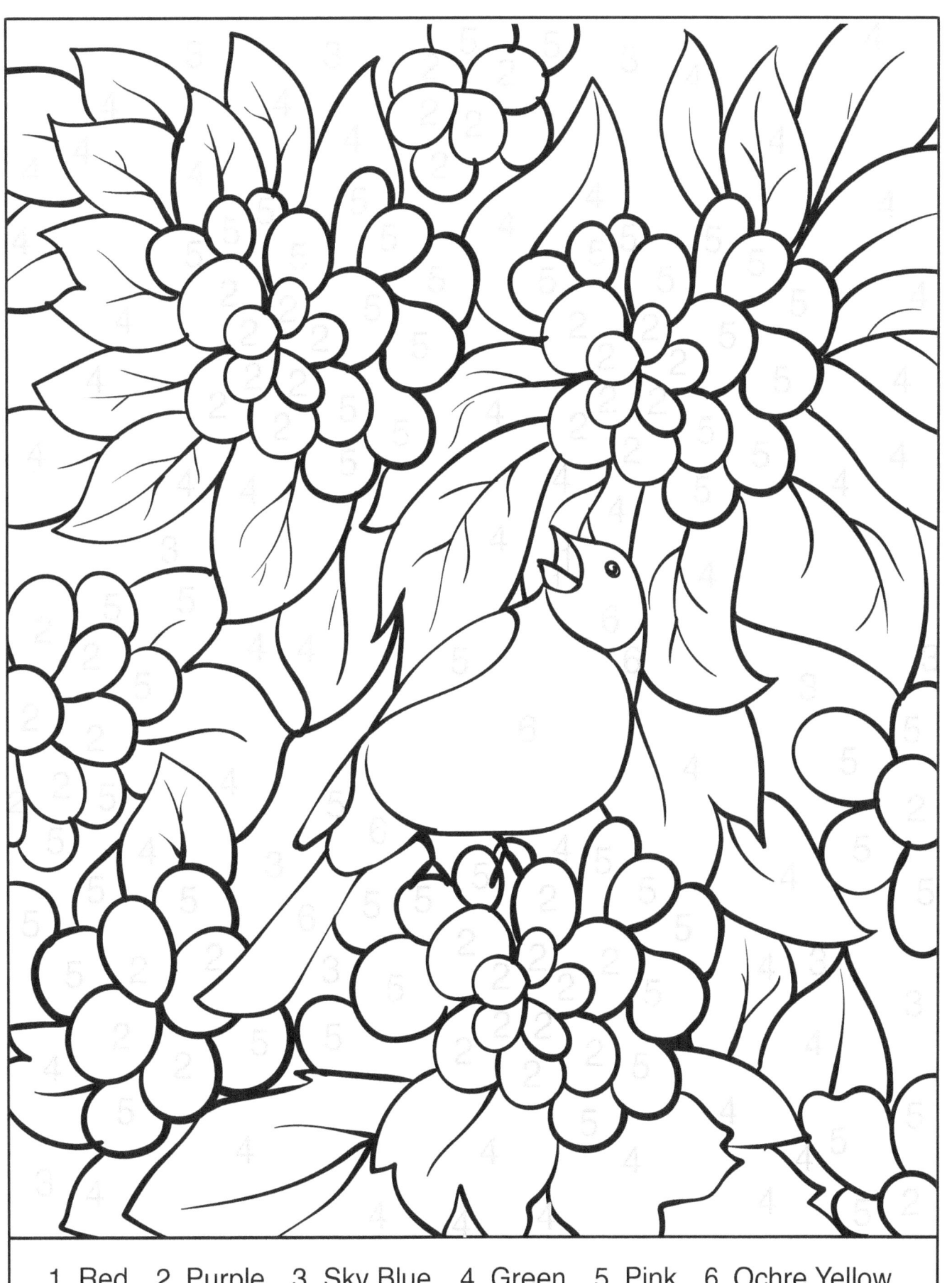

1. Red   2. Purple   3. Sky Blue   4. Green   5. Pink   6. Ochre Yellow

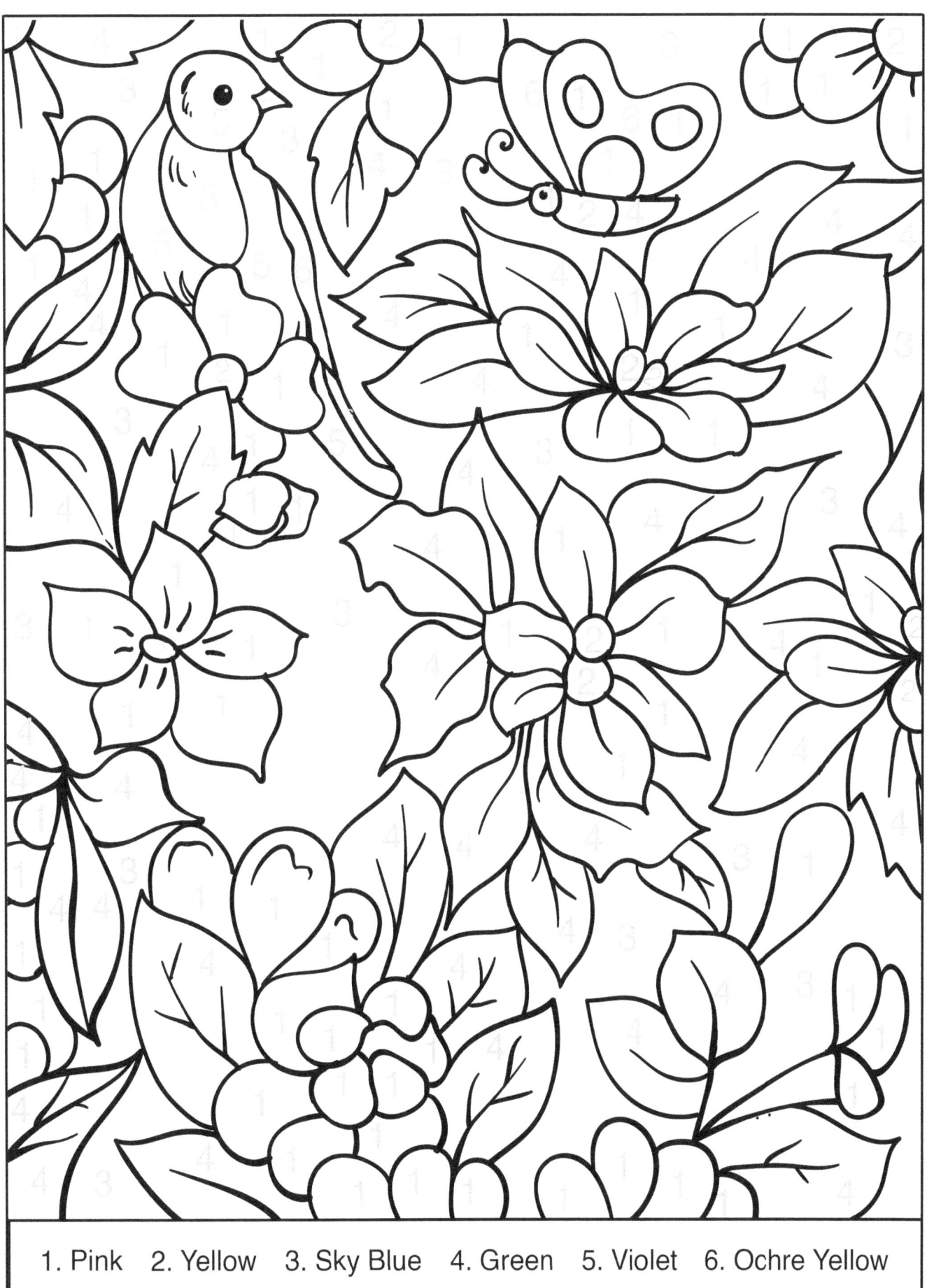

1. Pink   2. Yellow   3. Sky Blue   4. Green   5. Violet   6. Ochre Yellow

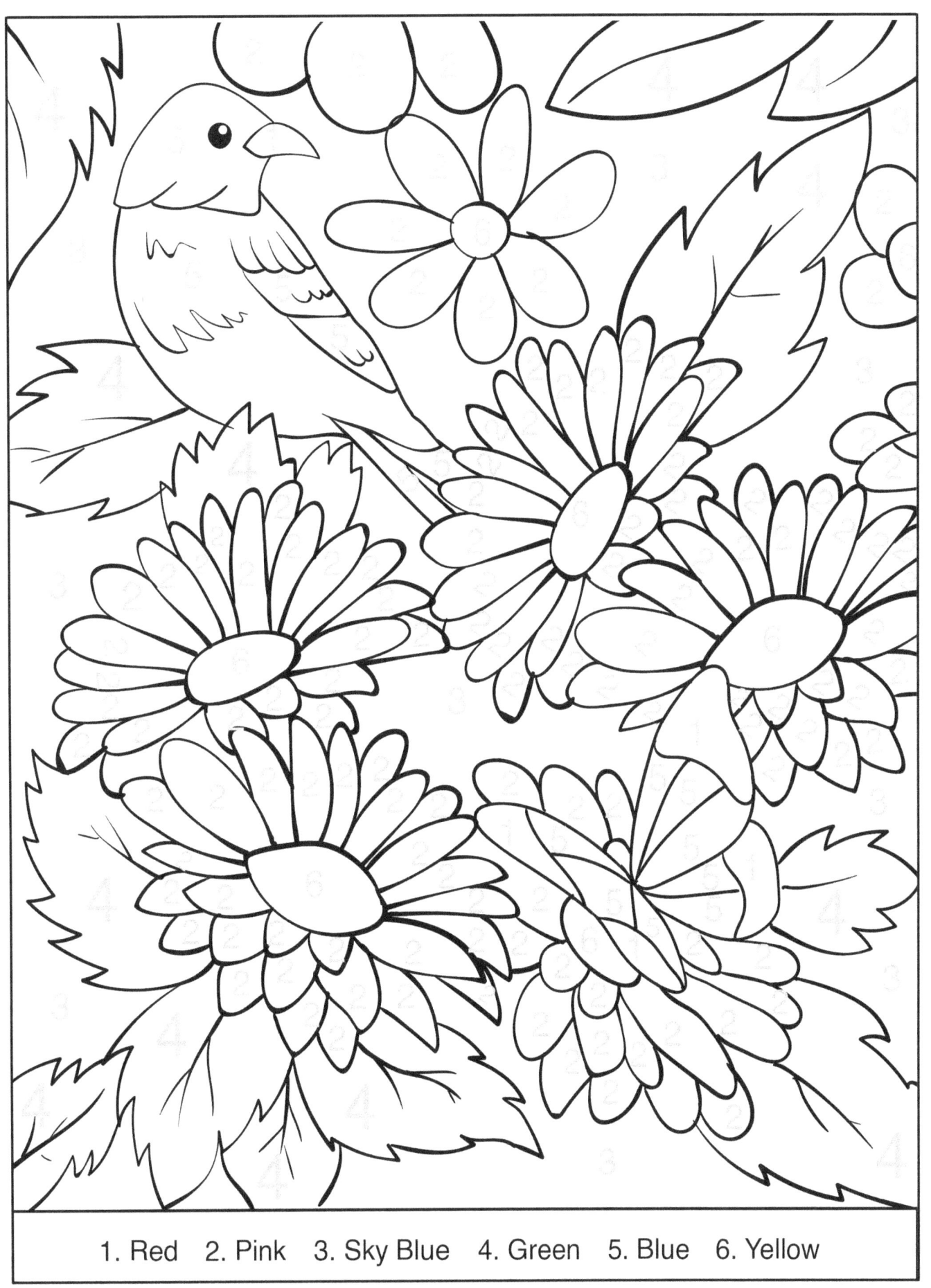

1. Red   2. Pink   3. Sky Blue   4. Green   5. Blue   6. Yellow

1. Red   2. Violet   3. Sky Blue   4. Green   5. Orange   6. Ochre Yellow

1. Orange   2. Yellow   3. Sky Blue   4. Green   5. Pink   6. Light Brown
7. Blue   8. Brown

1. Red   2. Light Pink   3. Pink   4. Dark Green   5. Sky Blue   6. Brown
7. Dark Pink   8. Yellow   9. Green

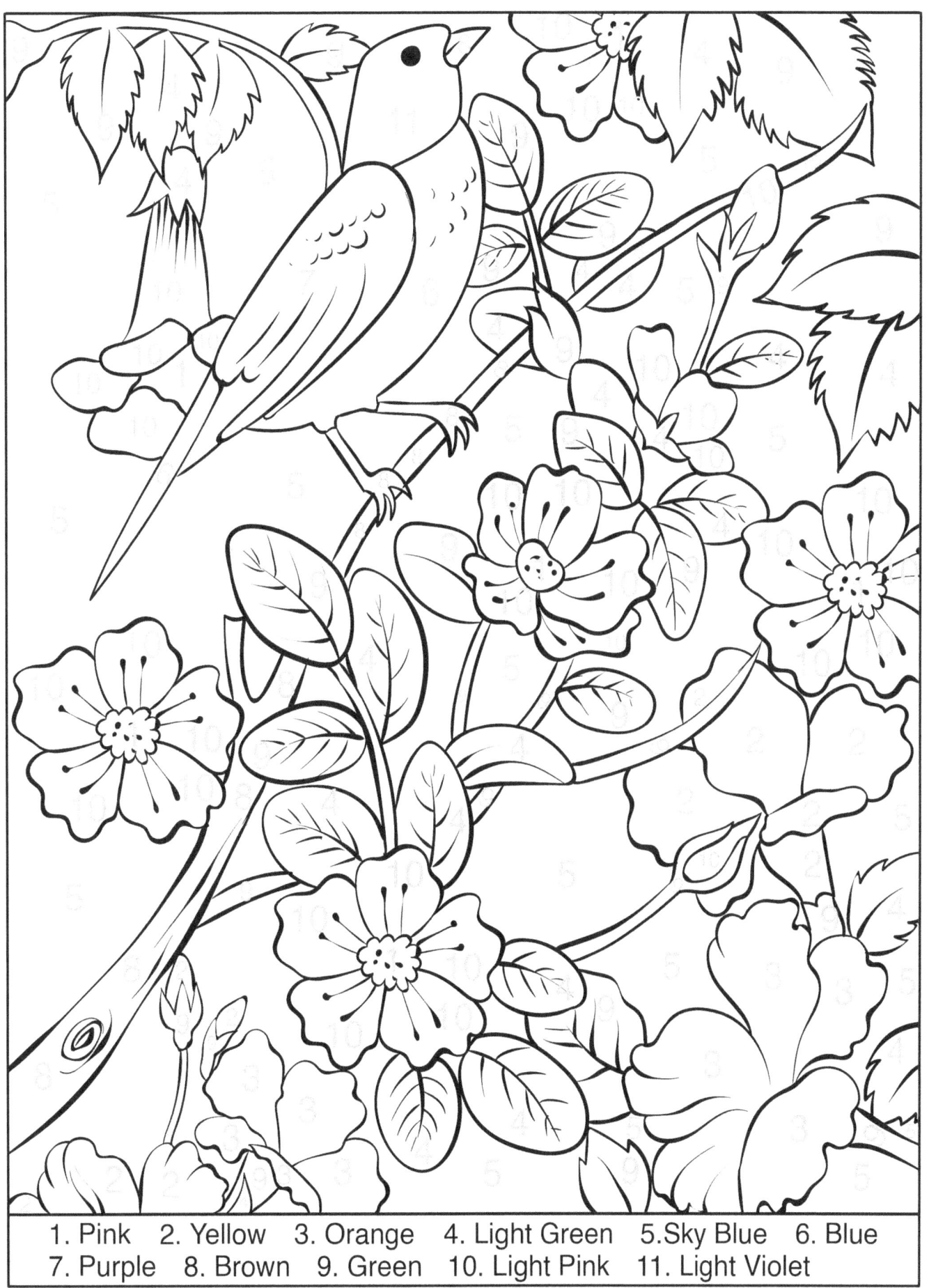

1. Pink   2. Yellow   3. Orange   4. Light Green   5.Sky Blue   6. Blue
7. Purple   8. Brown   9. Green   10. Light Pink   11. Light Violet

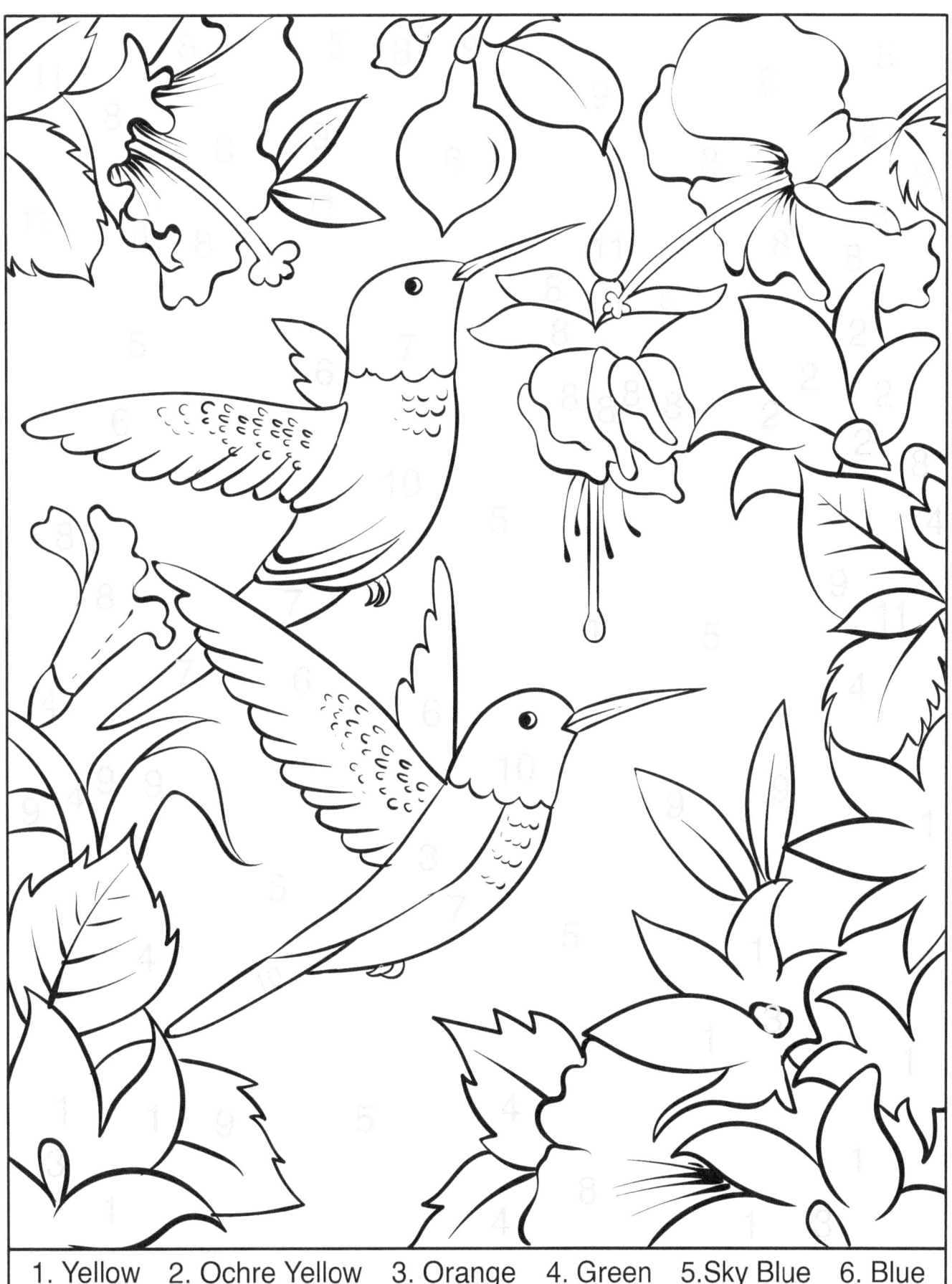

1. Yellow   2. Ochre Yellow   3. Orange   4. Green   5.Sky Blue   6. Blue
7. Violet   8. Pink   9. Green   10. Light Violet   11. Dark Green

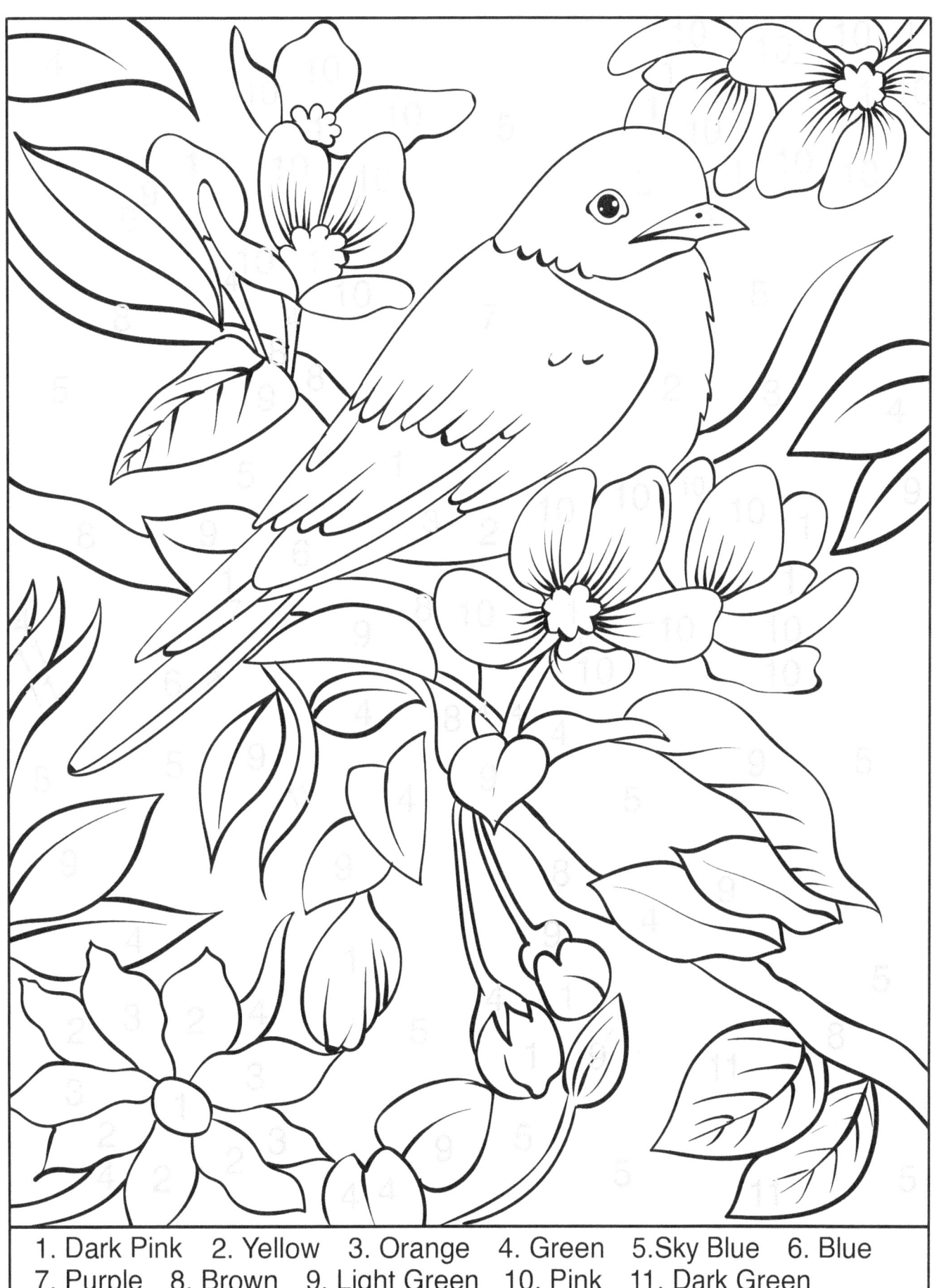

1. Dark Pink   2. Yellow   3. Orange   4. Green   5.Sky Blue   6. Blue
7. Purple   8. Brown   9. Light Green   10. Pink   11. Dark Green

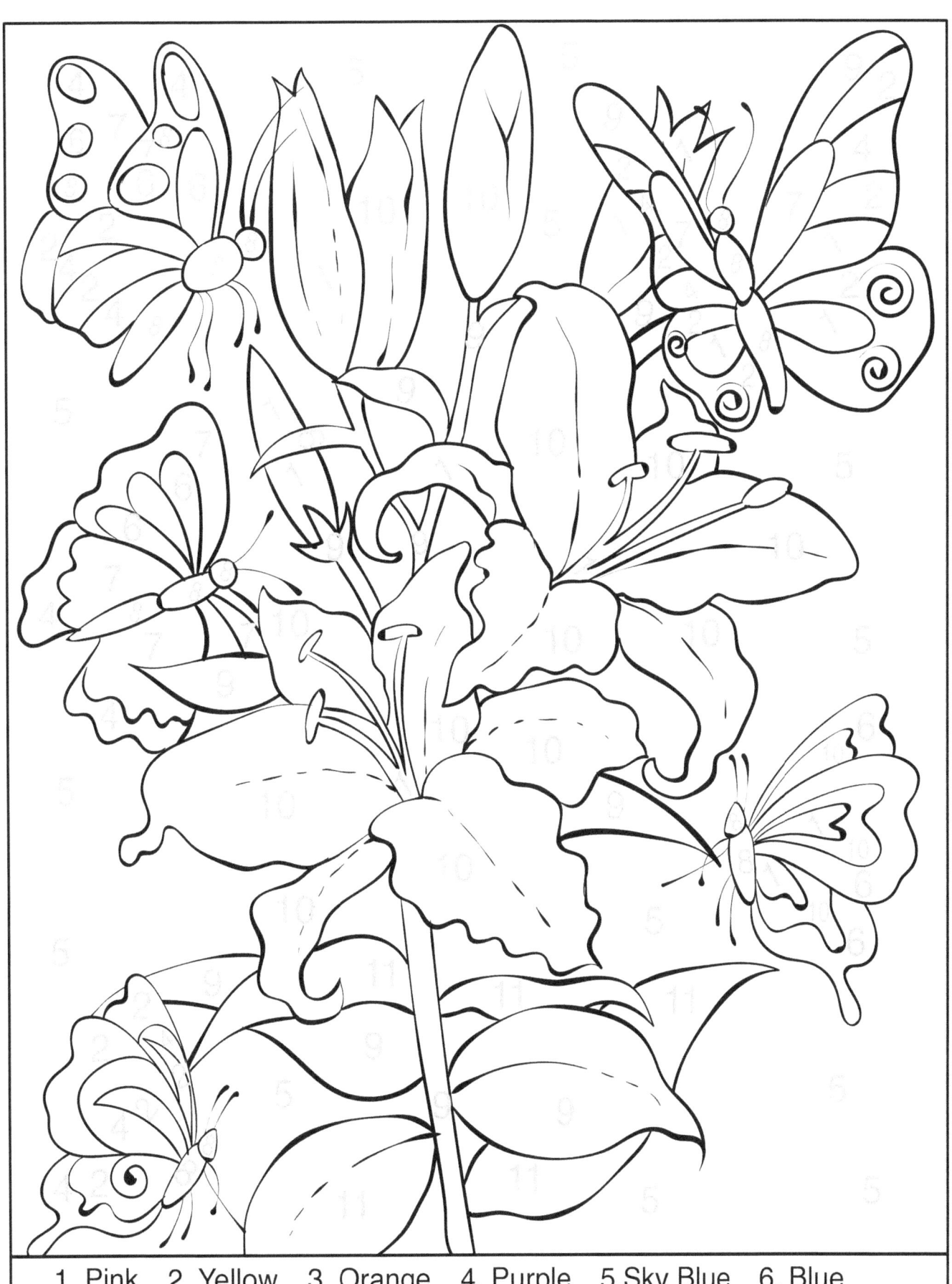

1. Pink   2. Yellow   3. Orange   4. Purple   5.Sky Blue   6. Blue
7. Light Brown   8. Brown   9. Green   10. LightPink   11. Light Green

# ENJOY BONUS IMAGES FROM SOME OF OUR OTHER FUN COLOR BY NUMBER BOOKS!

# FIND ALL OF OUR BOOKS ON AMAZON

Beautiful Cities and Landmarks
Color by Number
Mosaic World Geography
Coloring Book For Adults

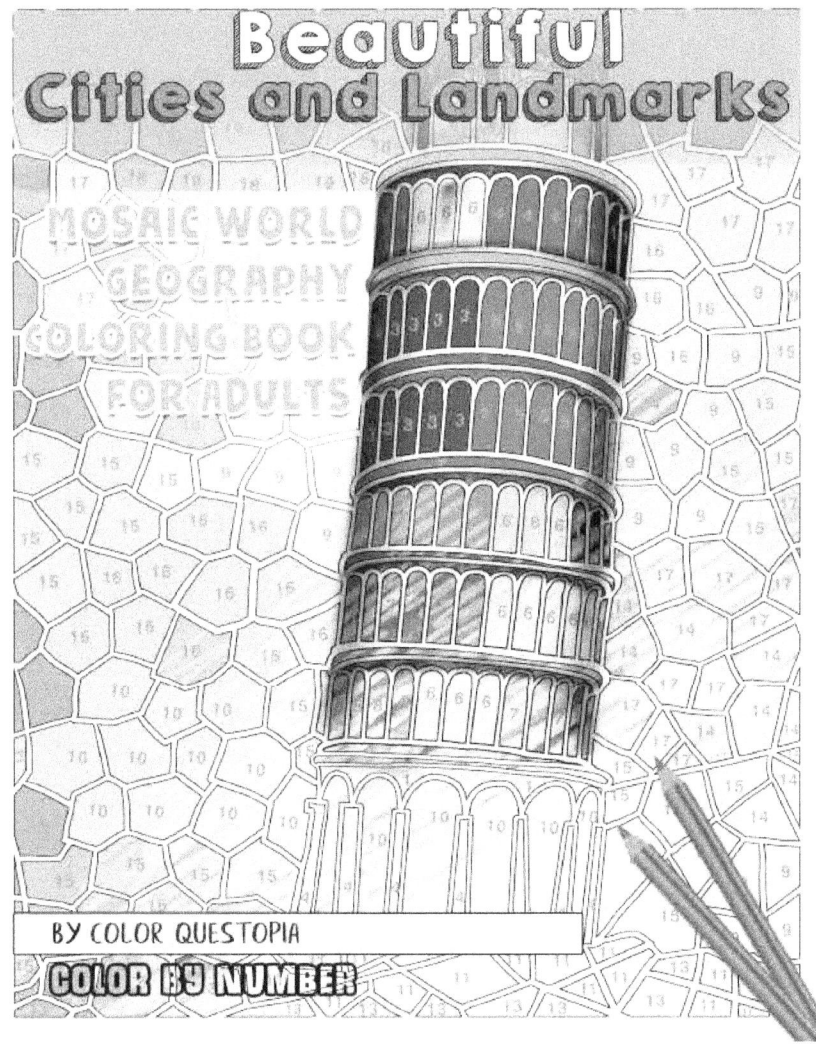

1. Light Green

2. Medium Green

3. Deep Green

4. Army Green

5. Brown

6. Light Brown

7. Dark Brown

8. Yellow

9. Blue

10. Violet

11. Orange

12. Beige

13. Pink

14. Dark Orange

15. Navy Blue

16. Neon Green

17. Baby Blue

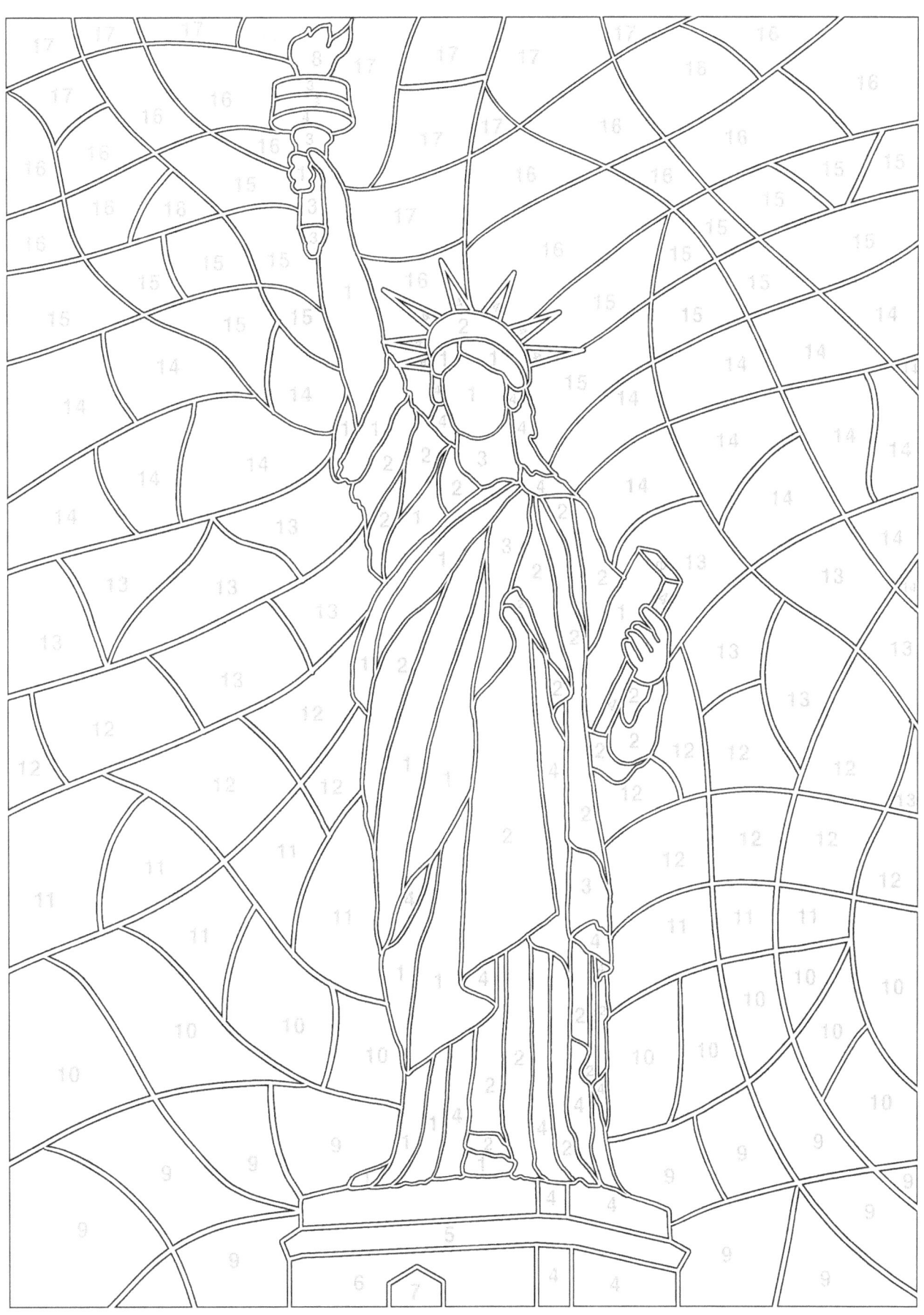

1. Black
2. Reddish Brown
3. Dark Brown
4. Light Brown
5. Golden Yellow
6. Yellow Ocher
7. Bronze
8. Sand Yellow
9. Light Yellow
10. Beige
11. Mustard Yellow
12. Dark Yellow
13. Sky Blue
14. Medium Blue
15. Light purple
16. Light pink
17. Pink
18. Royal Blue
19. Pale Turquoise
20. Violet

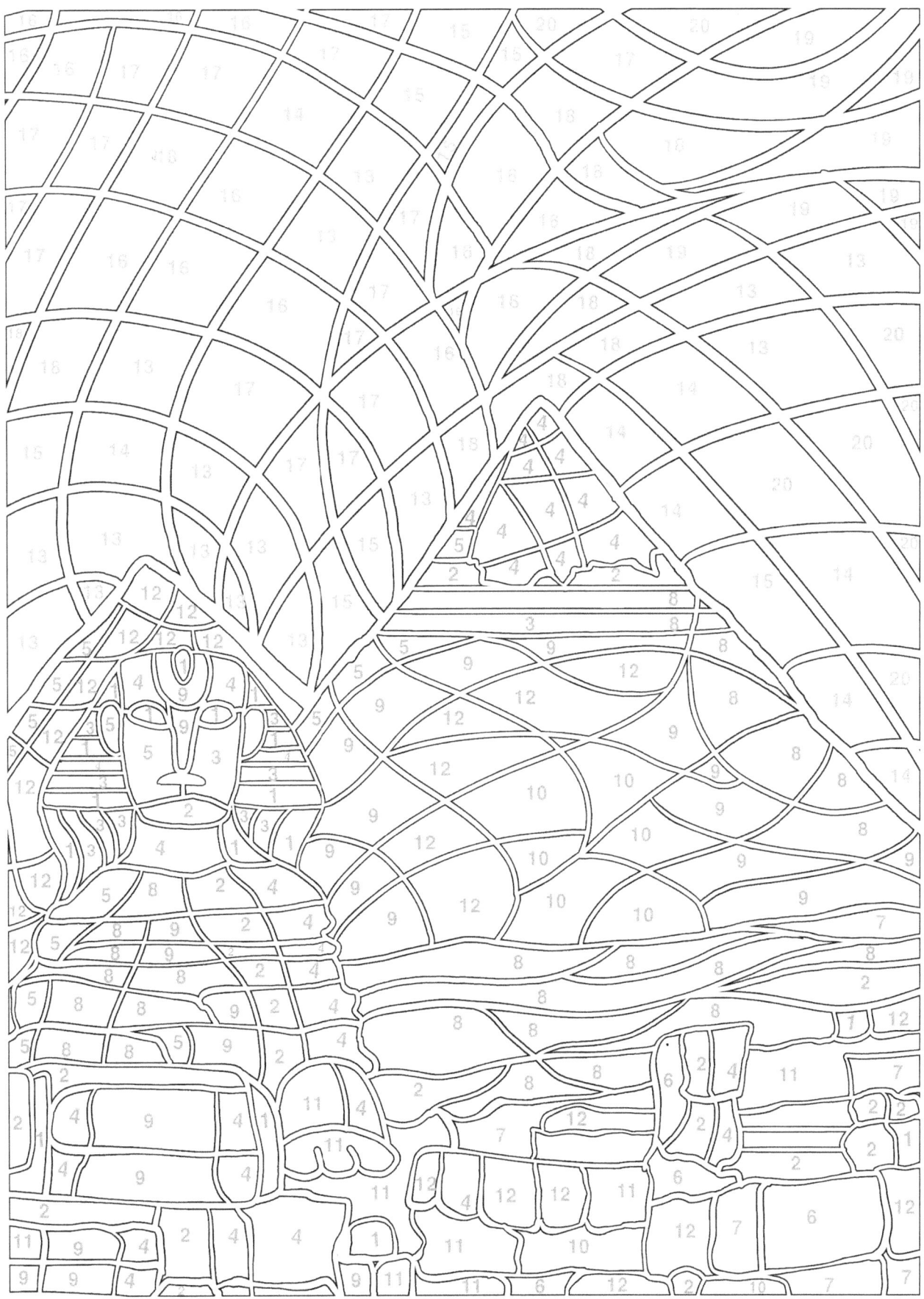

Country Farm Scenes
Nature, Animal, and Easy Designs
Adult Coloring Book
Color By Number For Adults

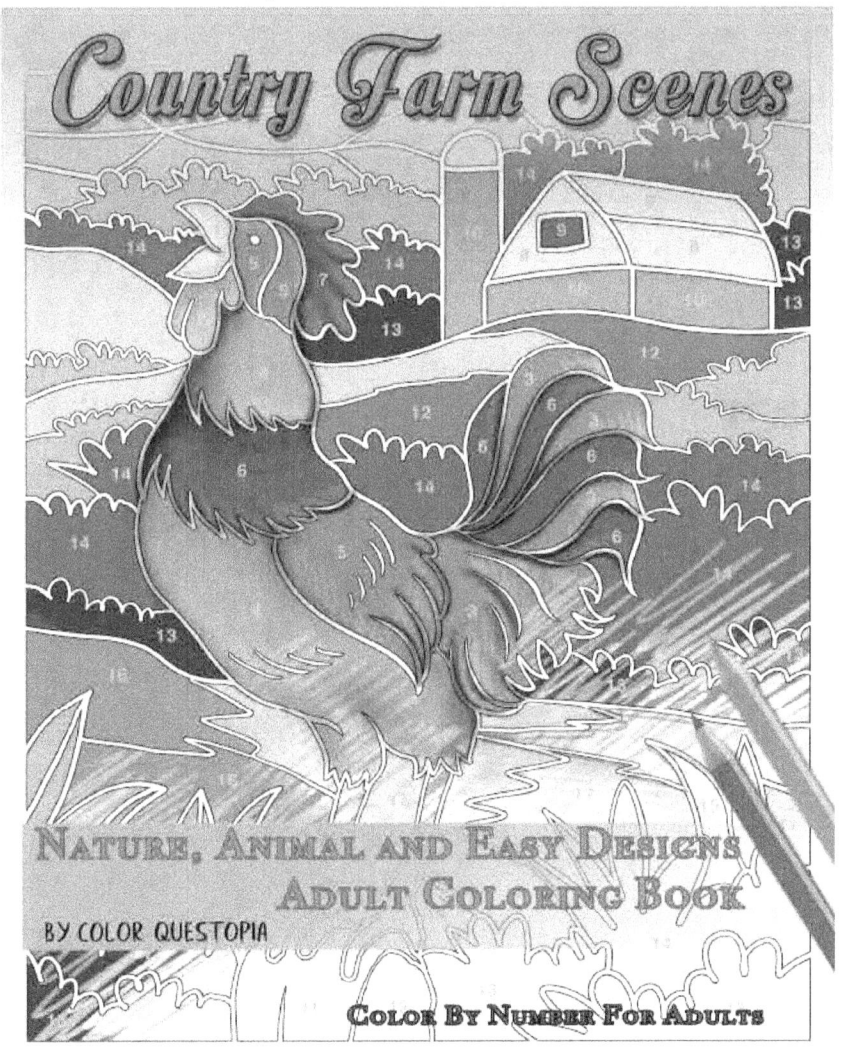

1. Orange
2. Dark Orange
3. Brown
4. Dark Yellow
5. Yellow
6. Red
7. Dark Red
8. Light Green
9. Dark Brown
10. Medium Brown
11. Dark Green
12. Green
13. Neon Green
14. Army Green
15. Light Brown
16. Blue
17. Sky Blue

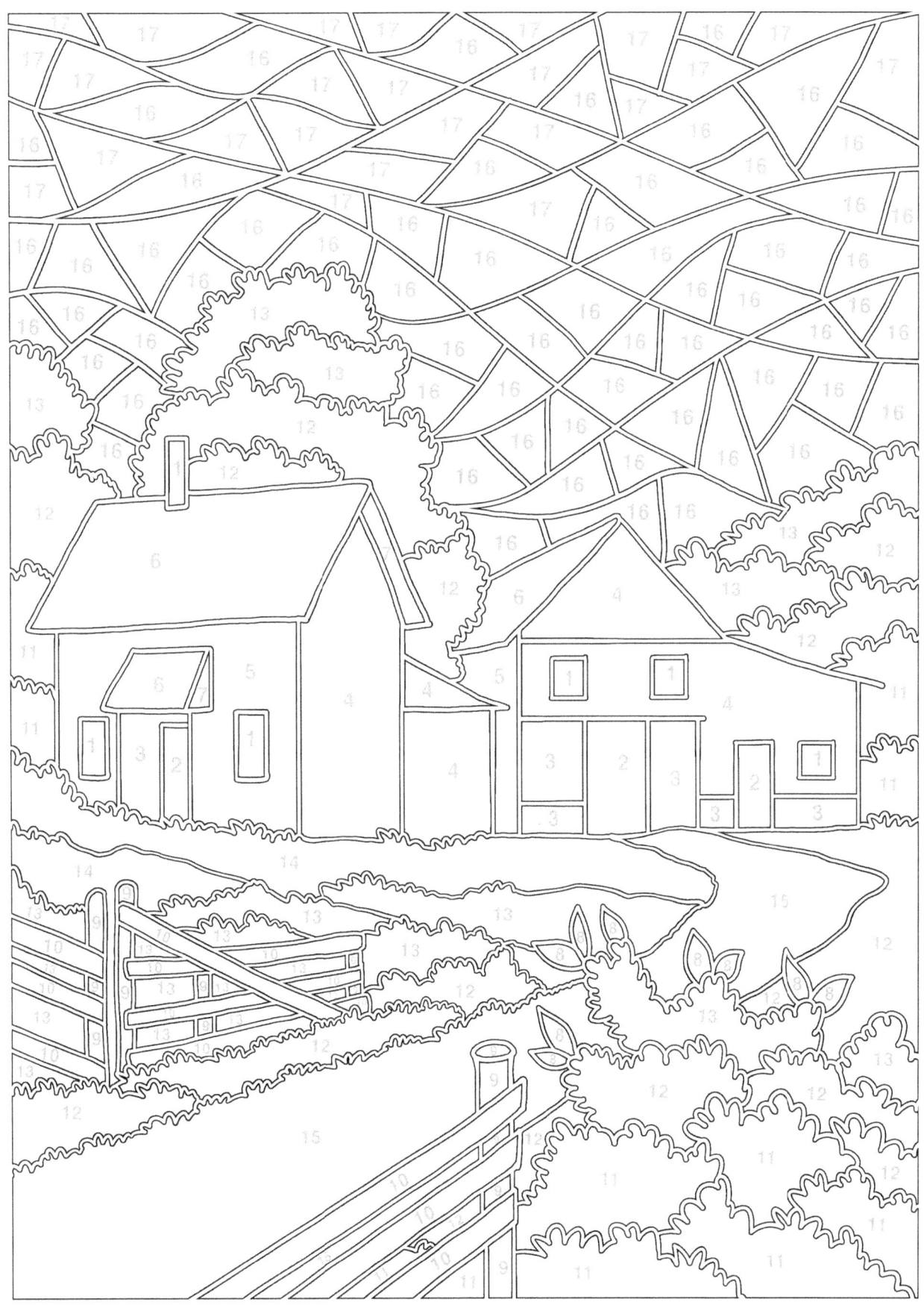

1. Black
2. Dark Brown
3. Light Pink
4. Dark Yellow
5. Brown
6. Green
7. Dark Green
8. Medium Green
9. Army Green
10. Neon Green
11. Light Green
12. Gray
13. Medium Gray
14. Light Gray
15. Blue
16. Navy Blue
17. Light Blue

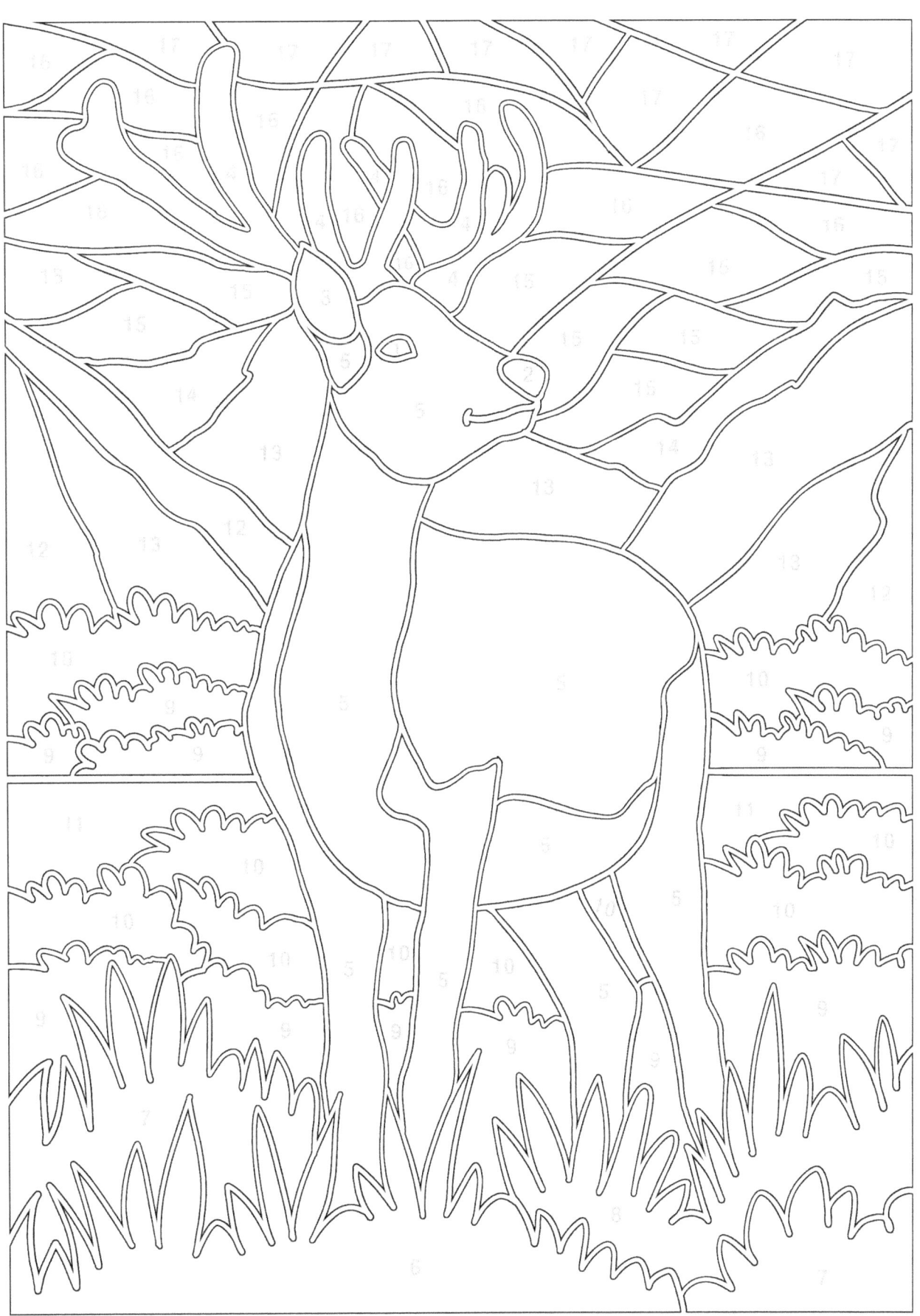

Horses Jumbo Adult Coloring Book
Horses and Ponies Grazing and Racing
Color by Number

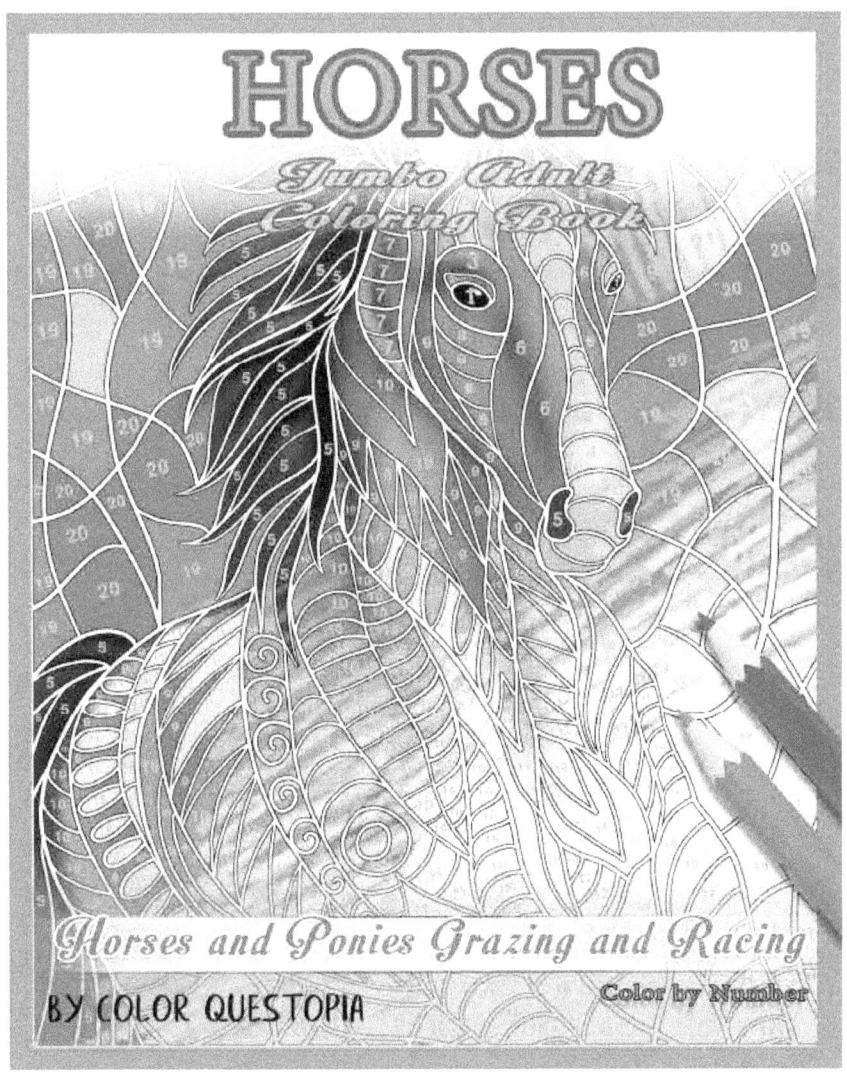

1. Dark Red
2. Brown
3. Dark Orange
4. Dark Brown
5. Orange
6. Light Gray
7. Light Red
8. Light Brown
9. Light Orange
10. Medium Brown
11. Yellow
12. Dark Gray
13. Light Gray
14. Light Orange
15. Blue
16. Sky Blue
17. Navy Blue
18. Light Blue

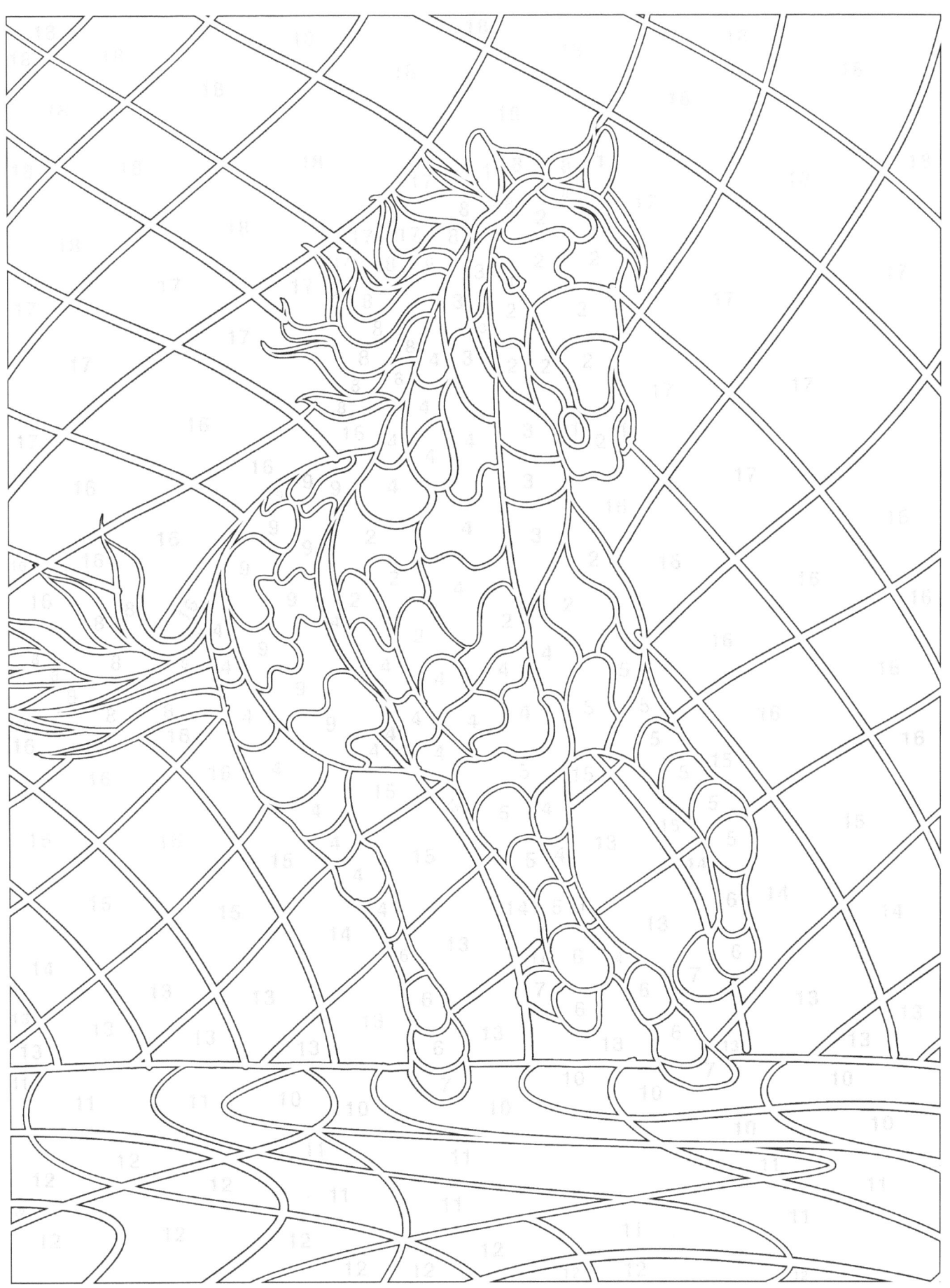

1. Black

2. Brown

3. Dark Brown

4. Light Brown

5. Red

6. Light Yellow

7. Dark Yellow

8. Dark Red

9. Gray

10. Light Gray

11. Medium Purple

12. Soft Violet

13. Dark Blue

14. Medium Green

15. Light Green

16. Deep Green

17. Dark Yellow

18. Yellow

19. Orange

20. Light Orange

21. Pink

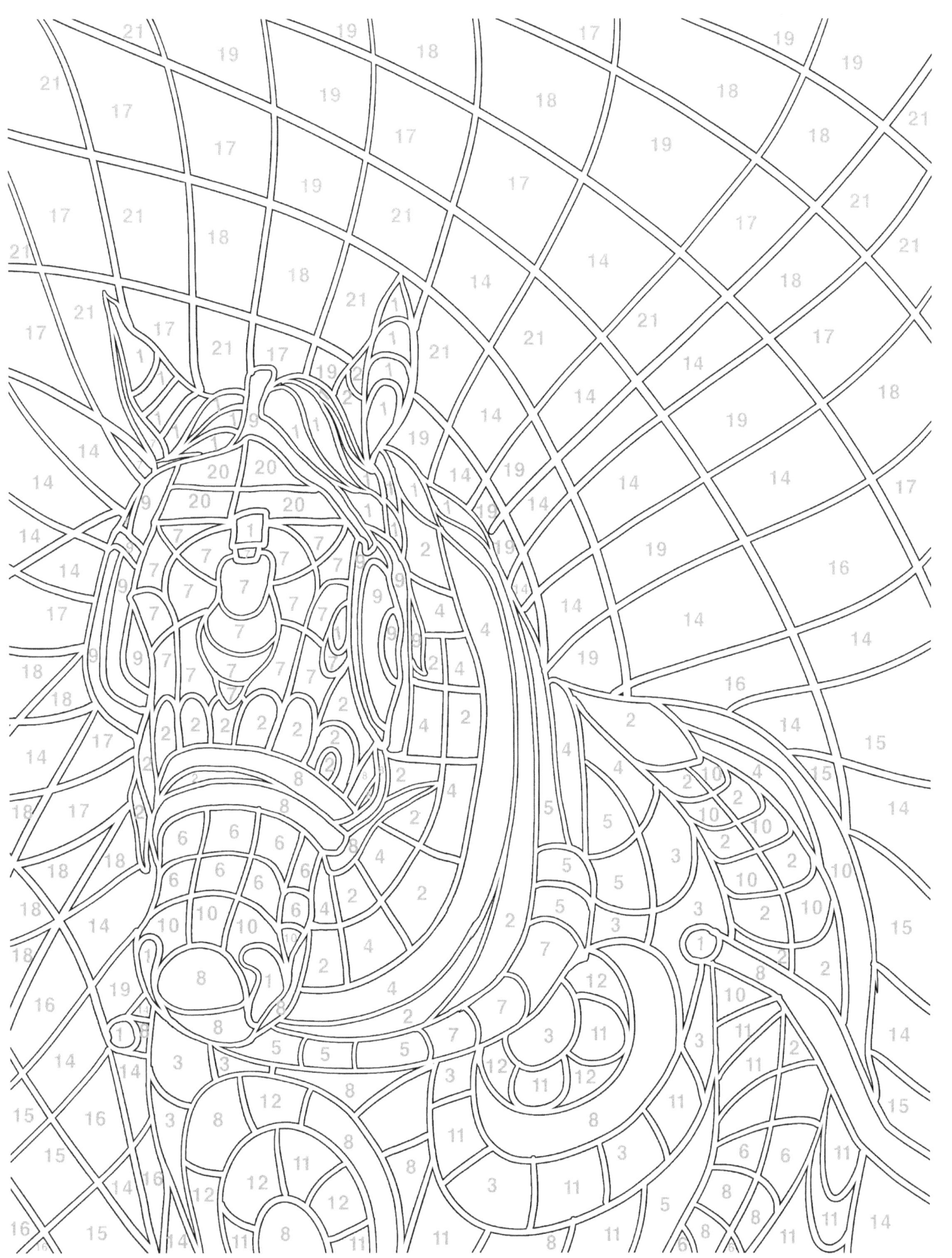

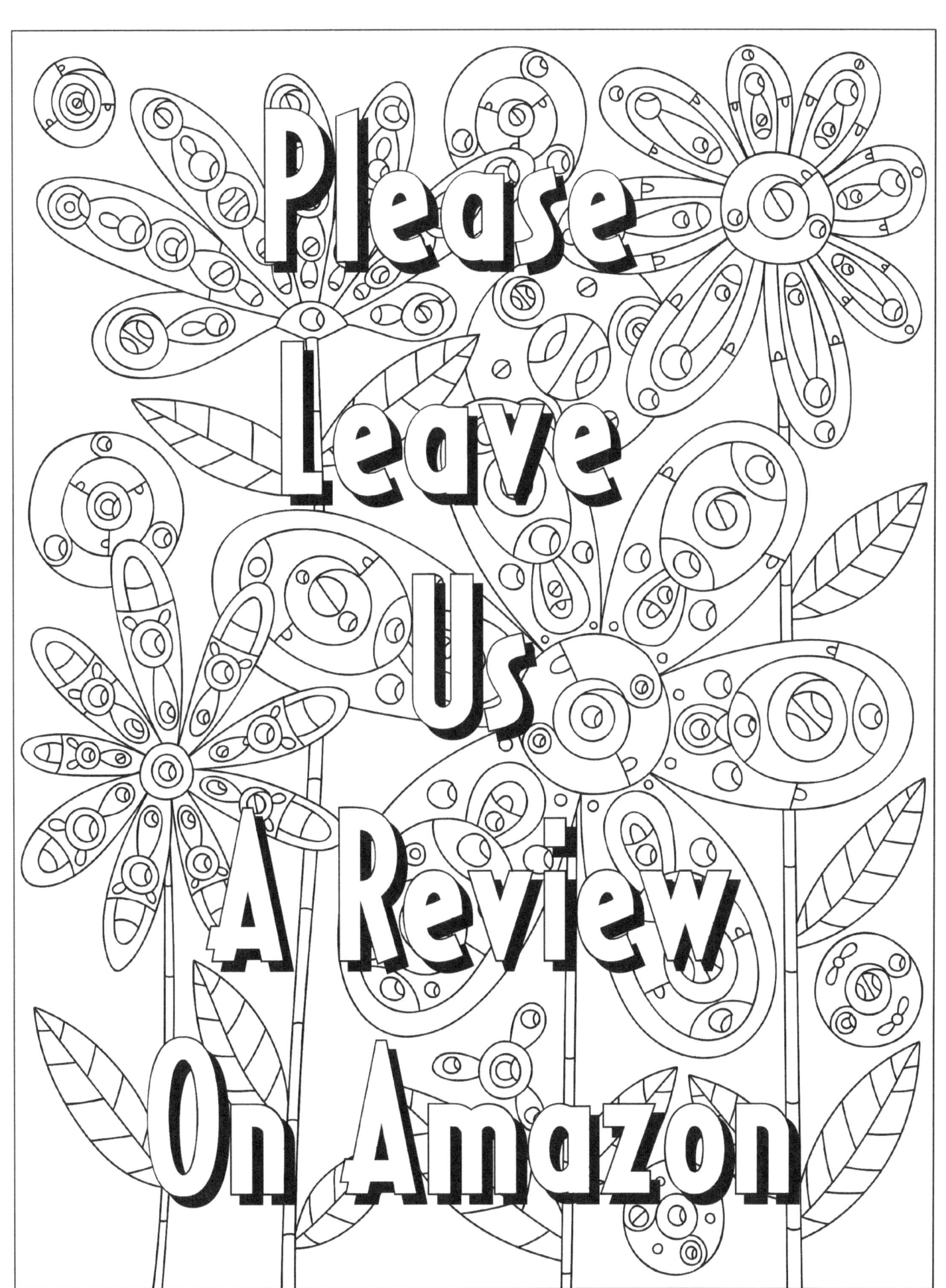

www.ingramcontent.com/pod-product-compliance
Lightning Source LLC
Chambersburg PA
CBHW080900220526
45467CB00008B/2579